SCHIRMER'S LIBRARY
OF MUSICAL CLASSICS

Vol. 1610

SERGEI RACHMANINOFF

Op. 30

Third Concerto

For the Piano

The Orchestra Accompaniment
Arranged for a Second Piano

ISBN 978-0-634-00616-6

G. SCHIRMER, Inc.

DISTRIBUTED BY

HAL•LEONARD®
CORPORATION
7777 W. BLUEMOUND RD. P.O. BOX 13819 MILWAUKEE, WI 53213

Third Concerto

Sergei Rachmaninoff, Op. 30

I

Più vivo

20

II
Intermezzo

III
Finale

Piano II

Piano II